The Ultimate
Coffee Quiz Book

The Ultimate Coffee Quiz Book

Master Coffee Drinks, Flavor, Roasting, Taste, Grinding, Testing, and More with Engaging Multiple-Choice Challenges!

Mohammed Al-Jaro

The Ultimate Coffee Quiz Book:

Master Coffee Drinks, Flavor, Roasting, Taste, Grinding, Testing, and More with Engaging Multiple-Choice Challenges!

ISBN: 979-8-218-50574-5

Contents

Introduction

Welcome to *The Ultimate Coffee Quiz* Book! This book is tailored for everyone—whether you're an experienced barista, a master roaster, a café owner, a dedicated coffee farmer, or simply someone who loves a good cup of coffee, there's something here for you. It aims to test your knowledge and enhance your appreciation for coffee. Within these pages, you'll encounter various captivating multiple-choice questions that explore different facets of coffee—drinks, flavors, roasting, and more. This book features 200 multiple-choice questions, each designed to challenge your expertise and ignite your curiosity about the fascinating world of coffee. Prepare to immerse yourself in coffee's diverse and rich realm and uncover how well you truly know it!

How to Use This Book

Welcome to *The Ultimate Coffee Quiz Book*! Here's how to get the most out of your coffee quiz experience:

1. Dive In: Start with any section that piques your interest. Each section covers a different aspect of coffee, so feel free to explore based on your preferences or curiosity.

2. Challenge Yourself: Use the multiple-choice questions to test your knowledge. Don't worry if you don't get all the answers right on your first try—learning is part of the fun!

3. Review: After answering the questions, read the provided short explanations.

4. Keep Track: Consider using a notebook or the space provided in the book to jot down any new facts or thoughts you have about coffee. This can help reinforce your learning and track your progress.

5. Have Fun: Most importantly, enjoy the process! Coffee is a diverse and fascinating subject, and this book is here to make your exploration as enjoyable as possible.

Additional Resources

If you're eager to dive deeper into the world of coffee, here are some recommended books and websites that can enhance your knowledge and appreciation:

Books:

- *The World Atlas of Coffee: From Beans to Brewing* by James Hoffmann – A comprehensive guide covering coffee's global journey, from bean to cup. Amazon Link (https://www.amazon.com/World-Atlas-Coffee-Explored-Explained/dp/1770854703)

- *Coffee: A Comprehensive Guide to the Bean, the Beverage, and the Process* by Robert W. Thurston – Detailed exploration of coffee's cultural, economic, and scientific aspects. Amazon Link (https://www.amazon.com/Coffee-Comprehensive-Guide-Beverage-Industry/dp/1442214406)

- *Coffee Obsession* by Anette Moldvaer – Practical advice on coffee varieties, brewing techniques, and equipment. Amazon Link (https://www.amazon.com/Coffee-Obsession-Anette-Moldvaer/dp/1409354687)

- *The Coffee Roaster's Companion* by Scott Rao – In-depth resource on the art and science of coffee roasting. Amazon Link (https://www.amazon.com/Coffee-Roasters-Companion-Scott-2014-05-04/dp/B01FGOH0AW)

Websites:

- **Specialty Coffee Association (SCA)** – Specialty Coffee Association (https://sca.coffee/).

- **National Coffee Association (NCA)** – National Coffee Association (https://www.ncausa.org/).

- **Coffee Review** – Coffee Review (https://www.coffeereview.com/).

- **Perfect Daily Grind** – Perfect Daily Grind (https://perfectdailygrind.com/).

- **Coffee Science** – Coffee Science (https://www.coffeescience.org/).

Author's Note

Hello, coffee lovers!

I'm Mohammed Ismail Al-Jaro, and my journey with coffee has been nothing short of an adventure. From the moment I first brewed my cup of coffee, I was captivated by the intricate flavors, the rich history, and the art of brewing. My passion for coffee led me to explore every facet of this remarkable beverage.

Creating *The Ultimate Coffee Quiz Book* has been a labor of love. I wanted to craft a resource that not only challenges your coffee knowledge but also fuels your curiosity and passion for coffee. Whether you're a seasoned barista, a dedicated roaster, or a casual coffee drinker, I hope this book sparks a deeper appreciation for the world of coffee and inspires you to continue your coffee journey.

Thank you for joining me on this adventure. May your coffee always be delicious and your knowledge ever-expanding!

Feedback Section

Your feedback is invaluable! If you have any thoughts, suggestions, or comments about *The Ultimate Coffee Quiz Book*, I'd love to hear from you. Your input helps me improve and create better resources for coffee enthusiasts like you.

How to Provide Feedback:

- Email: Drop me an email at aljaromohammed@gmail.com with your feedback.

- Leave a review for this eBook on the site you purchased it from.

Thank you for being a part of this coffee journey!

Disclaimer:

"All of the multiple-choice questions in this book have been inspired by and adapted from *A Coffee Lover's Guide to Coffee: All the Must-Know Coffee Methods, Techniques, Equipment, Ingredients and Secrets by* Shlomo Stern (https://www.amazon.com/Shlomo-Stern/e/B0195515R2/ref=dp_byline_cont_ebooks_1). The questions are based on the scientific data provided in the original work. Every effort has been made to present this information accurately while drawing on the valuable insights from the original source."

Quiz Content

1-A. Coffee Drinks

1. Which type of Espresso is made with 0.25 Oz (7 grams) of ground coffee and served in a small cup?

    A. Lungo

    B. Double or Doppio

    C. Quad

    D. Basic Shot (Short Black)

2. What is the ideal time to produce a Shot of Espresso?

    A. 25 Sec

    B. 40 Sec

    C. 45 Sec

    D. 50 Sec

3. What type of Espresso is made by adding extra water to a basic shot of Espresso that contains 0.25 Oz (7 grams) of ground coffee?

    A. Lungo

    B. Double or Doppio

    C. Quad

    D. Basic Shot

4. The extraction time for a Lungo is increased to _____ to produce approximately 45 to 60 ml of the beverage.

    A. 25-30 sec

    B. 30-35 sec

    C. 45-55 sec

    D. 50-55 sec

5. What is the name of the drink that results from two Espresso shots using 0.5 Oz (14 grams) of ground coffee, producing about 1.7-2.2 oz (50-65 ml) of liquid?

    A. Lungo

    B. Double or Doppio

    C. Quad

    D. Ristretto

6. Adding a small piece of lemon peel to a short Espresso creates which type of drink?

    A. Double or Doppio

    B. Ristretto

    C. Espresso Romano

    D. Quad

7. Dropping the lemon peel into an Espresso reduces the coffee's _____.

    A. Bitterness

    B. Sweetness

    C. Sourness

    D. Saltiness

8. What is the beverage called that combines one shot of Espresso with steamed and frothed milk?

    A. Long Black

    B. Cappuccino

    C. Americano

    D. Café Breve

9. What is the name of the diluted drink made by pouring a single Espresso shot into a 6/7 Oz (180-210 ml) glass and adding hot water?

    A. Long Black

    B. Cappuccino

    C. Americano

    D. Café Breve

10. What is the name of the Espresso-based drink made with hot water, where Espresso is poured over two-thirds of a 6-7 oz (180-200ml) cup of hot water to preserve the crema?

    A. Long Black

    B. Cappuccino

    C. Americano

    D. Café Breve

11. What is the name of the drink where a short Espresso is poured into a cup, and steamed half-and-half is added, resulting in a creamier beverage with more fat?

    A. Long Black

    B. Cappuccino

    C. Americano

    D. Café Breve

12. What is the name of the drink made from a single or double Espresso topped with whipped sweet cream?

    A. Long Black

    B. Espresso Con Panna

    C. Americano

    D. Café Breve

13. What is the name of the drink made with a short Espresso topped with one tablespoon of frothed milk, creating a white spot on a brown surface?

A. Macchiato

B. Espresso Con Panna

C. Americano

D. Café Breve

14. What is the name of the coffee drink that is brewed with cold water over an extended period, resulting in a smooth, less acidic flavor, and typically served chilled?

A. Iced Latte

B. Cold Brew

C. Frappuccino

D. Iced Americano

15. Which drink is the opposite of a Macchiato, featuring a brown spot on a white background?

A. Flat White

B. Latte Macchiato

C. Latte

D. Café Breve

16. What is the smaller version of a cappuccino that contains less milk?

A. Macchiato

B. Latte Macchiato

C. Latte

D. Piccolo Latte

17. The Piccolo Latte is most commonly found in which country, having recently spread to other parts of the world?

    A. Australia

    B. Spain

    C. Brazil

    D. Russia

18. In some regions of Spain, what is the Piccolo Latte referred to as?

    A. Latte

    B. Cortado

    C. Flat white

    D. Macchiato

19. Which coffee beverage is similar to a latte but with a different Espresso-to-milk ratio, featuring less milk and foam?

    A. Macchiato

    B. Piccolo Latte

    C. Flat white

    D. Espresso Con Panna

20. If someone needs to stay awake and requires extra caffeine, which drink, combining a cup of filtered coffee with a shot of Espresso, might they ask for?

    A. Latte

    B. Piccolo Latte

    C. Flat white

    D. Red Eye

21. What is the most commonly served coffee in France, made by pouring a half-cup of filtered coffee into a 3-5 oz (100-150 ml) glass and adding hot milk?

    A. Red Eye

    B. Café Au Lait

    C. Flat white

    D. Cortado

22. What is the most popular coffee served in Austria, made with filtered coffee, cream, and chocolate flakes sprinkled on top?

    A. Wiener Mélange

    B. Café Au Lait

    C. Flat white

    D. Cortado

23. What is the name of the coffee combined with chocolate?

    A. Café Mocha

    B. Café Au Lait

    C. Black Eye

    D. Cortado

24. _____ is an Italian dessert beverage that features a combination of Espresso and ice cream.

    A. Cortado

    B. Affogato

    C. Café Mocha

    D. Café Au Lait

25. In what way does the texture of the milk in a Flat White differ from that in a Cappuccino?

A. Flat White milk has more foam when steamed compared to Cappuccino milk.

B. Flat White milk is smoother and less frothy than Cappuccino milk.

C. Cappuccino milk is steamed to a thinner consistency than Flat White milk.

D. Cappuccino milk is more textured and has a thicker layer of foam than Flat White milk.

1-B. Coffee Drink Questions Answers

1. Correct answer: D) Basic Shot (Short Black)

Description: The Basic Shot (Short Black) is prepared using 0.25 Oz (7 grams) of ground coffee and is served in a small cup.

2. Correct answer: A) 25 Sec

Description: A Shot of Espresso should be brewed in about 25 seconds.

3. Correct answer: A) Lungo

Description: The Lungo is prepared by adding more water to a basic shot of Espresso that uses 0.25 Oz (7 grams) of ground coffee.

4. Correct answer: C) 45-55 sec

Description: The extraction time for a Lungo is extended to 45-55 seconds to yield about 45 to 60 ml of the beverage.

5. Correct answer: B) Double or Doppio

Description: A) Double or Doppio is a drink made from two Espresso shots with 0.5 Oz (14 grams) of ground coffee, resulting in approximately 1.7-2.2 oz (50-65 ml) of liquid.

6. Correct answer: C) Espresso Romano

Description: A short Espresso becomes an Espresso Romano when a small piece of lemon peel is added.

7. Correct answer: A) Bitterness

Description: Adding the lemon peel into an Espresso decreases the coffee's bitterness.

8. Correct answer: B) Cappuccino

Description: A Cappuccino is a drink that combines one shot of Espresso with steamed and frothed milk.

9. Correct answer: C) Americano

Description: An Americano is a diluted drink made by pouring a single shot of Espresso into a 6/7 Oz (180-210 ml) glass and adding hot water.

10. Correct answer: A) Long Black

Description: A Long Black is an Espresso-based beverage where Espresso is poured over two-thirds of a 6-7 oz (180-200ml) cup of hot water to maintain the crema.

11. Correct answer: D) Café Breve

Description: The drink where a short Espresso is poured into a cup and steamed half-and-half is added, resulting in a creamier beverage with more fat, is called a Café Breve.

12. Correct answer: B) Espresso Con Panna

Description: When topping a single or double Espresso with whipped sweet, this drink is called Espresso Con Panna.

13. Correct answer: A) Macchiato

Description: A Macchiato is a short Espresso topped with one tablespoon of frothed milk, forming a white spot on a brown surface.

14. Correct answer: B) Cold Brew

Description: Cold Brew is made by putting coarsly grounded coffee in cold water for 12 to 24 hours, which produce a smooth, less acidic drink.

15. Correct answer: B) Latte Macchiato

Description: A Latte Macchiato is the reverse of a Macchiato, with a brown spot on a white background.

16. Correct answer: D) Piccolo Latte

Description: A Piccolo Latte is a smaller version of a cappuccino, containing less milk.

17. Correct answer: A) Australia

Description: The Piccolo Latte is a popular drink in Australia that has recently gained popularity globally.

18. Correct answer: B) Cortado

Description: The Piccolo Latte is known as a Cortado in certain regions of Spain.

19. Correct answer: C) Flat white

Description: The Flat White is similar to a latte, but with a different Espresso-to-milk ratio, containing less milk and foam.

20. Correct answer: D) Red Eye

Description: A Red Eye is a combination of a cup of filtered coffee with a shot of Espresso, often requested by those needing extra caffeine to stay awake.

21. Correct answer: B) Café Au Lait

Description: The Café Au Lait is the most popular coffee served in France, made by pouring a half-cup of filtered coffee into a 3-5 oz (100-150 ml) glass and adding hot milk.

22. Correct answer: A) Wiener Mélange

Description: The Wiener Mélange is the most popular coffee in Austria, made with filtered coffee, cream, and chocolate flakes sprinkled on top.

23. Correct answer: A) Café Mocha

Description: A Café Mocha is a coffee mixed with chocolate.

24. Correct answer: B) Affogato

Description: An Affogato is an Italian dessert drink made by pairing Espresso with ice cream.

25. Correct answer: B) Flat White milk is smoother and less frothy than Cappuccino milk.

Description: The milk in a Flat White has a smoother texture and is less frothy than the milk in a Cappuccino.

Notes:

....
....
....
....
....
....
....
....
....
....
....
....
....
....
....
....
....
....
....
....
....
....
....
....

2-A. Coffee Flavor by Country

1. The coffee from _____ is known for its pleasant aroma, rich fragrance, medium-heavy body, and delicate acidity.

    A. Brazil

    B. Bolivia

    C. Colombia

    D. Cameroon

2. The coffee from _____ is recognized for its heavy body, strong aroma, medium to high acidity, smooth texture, and a pleasant aftertaste that lingers.

    A. Costa Rica

    B. Bolivia

    C. Burundi

    D. Cameroon

3. The coffee from _____ shares similarities with Mexican coffee, having medium acidity, body, and aroma. It has a soft taste that fades quickly.

    A. Costa Rica

    B. El Salvador

    C. Burundi

    D. Cameroon

4. The coffee from _____ is noted for its good acidity, fruity flavor, and balanced body.

    A. Brazil

    B. Bolivia

    C. Burundi

    D. Ethiopia

5. The coffee from _____ is sweeter and less acidic compared to other Central American coffees.

    A. Brazil

    B. Kenya

    C. Costa Rica

    D. Colombia

6. The coffee from _____ offers a medium body, good acidity, and a slightly bitter chocolate flavor with a smoky undertone.

    A. Costa Rica

    B. Guatemala

    C. Ethiopia

    D. Ecuador

7. The coffee from _____ has a medium body and good acidity, with an excellent aftertaste that lingers long after consumption.

    A. Hawaii

    B. Guatemala

    C. Ethiopia

    D. India

8. The coffee from _____ has a medium aroma, medium acidity, and a weak body.

    A. Hawaii

    B. Guatemala

    C. Honduras

    D. India

9. Monsoon coffee from _____ is known for its strong, pungent flavor.

    A. Hawaii

    B. Guatemala

    C. Honduras

    D. India

10. The coffee from _____ has a full body, low acidity, and a subtle earth and tree fragrance that lingers on the palate.

    A. Costa Rica

    B. India

    C. Indonesia

    D. Honduras

11. The coffee from _____ has a strong body, very low acidity, and a touch of bitterness that tingles on the tongue. However, the sweet grass aftertaste remains for a long time.

    A. Sulawesi - Indonesia

    B. Sumatra - Indonesia

    C. Java - Indonesia

    D. India

12. The coffee from _____ is rich with high acidity, a strong fragrance, medium body, and a hint of fruity aftertaste.

    A. Indonesia

    B. Jamaica

    C. Ivory Coast (Côte d'Ivoire)

    D. Kenya

13. The coffee from _____ has a medium body, medium acidity, and a nutty flavor.

    A. Kenya

    B. Mexico

    C. Nicaragua

    D. Panama

14. The coffee from _____ is well-balanced, with good acidity and a full body, enhanced by fruity sweetness.

    A. Kenya

    B. Mexico

    C. Nicaragua

    D. Panama

15. The best quality coffee from _____ is known for its high aroma, medium acidity, medium body, and fruity notes.

    A. Papua New Guinea

    B. Peru

    C. Mexico

    D. Panama

16. The coffee from _____ is typically African, with a medium body and strong acidity.

    A. Tanzania

    B. Ethiopia

    C. Uganda

    D. Rwanda

17. The Robusta coffee from _____ is vigorous, with a full body, lively acidity, and a unique sweetness.

    A. Tanzania

    B. Peru

    C. Uganda

    D. Rwanda

18. The coffee from _____ is low in acidity and has a strong aroma.

    A. Papua New Guinea

    B. Venezuela

    C. Uganda

    D. Vietnam

19. The coffee from _____ has a strong body, high acidity, and a rich aroma. It also has fruity and chocolatey notes with a hint of bitterness.

    A. Yemen

    B. Peru

    C. Uganda

    D. Rwanda

20. _____ coffee is rich, well-balanced, with a medium to full body, mild sweetness, good acidity, and a very pleasant aroma.

    A. Colombian Supremo

    B. El Salvador Adelaida

    C. Costa Rica Monte Crisol

    D. Guatemalan Huehuetenango

21. _____ coffee has subtle and mild fruit flavors, a light body, sweet fragrance, and a clean finish that lingers pleasantly.

    A. Guatemalan Huehuetenango

    B. El Salvador Adelaida

    C. Costa Rica Monte Crisol

    D. Colombian Supremo

22. _____ coffee has a complex, deep, earthy, and pungent profile with hints of dry cinnamon, cardamom, and dried fruits.

    A. El Salvador Adelaida

    B. Yemen Mocha

    C. Tanzania Peaberry

    D. Ethiopian Yirgacheffe

23. _____ coffee is bright, medium to light-bodied, with fruity berry undertones and distinct floral notes in the aroma.

    A. Nicaragua Segovia Organic

    B. Yemen Mocha

    C. Tanzania Peaberry

    D. Ethiopian Yirgacheffe

24. _____ coffee is known for its complex, intense, and earthy flavors, with a smooth, heavy body, sweet chocolate notes, low acidity, and a hint of licorice.

    A. Uganda Bugisi Organic

    B. Malawi Ngapani AAA

    C. Sumatra Mandheling

    D. Tanzania Hope AA Organic

25. _____ coffee has a well-balanced taste, dense body, flavors of pastries, plums, and cinnamon, with a rich aroma and bright citrus acidity.

A. Sumatra Lintong

B. Guatemala Antigua Estela Plus

C. El Salvador Adelaida

D. Colombian Excelso

2-B. Coffee Flavor by Country Questions Answers

1. Correct answer: C) Colombia

Description: Colombian coffee is renowned for its delightful aroma, rich fragrance, medium-heavy body, and delicate acidity.

2. Correct answer: A) Costa Rica

Description: Costa Rican coffee is characterized by a heavy body, strong aroma, medium to high acidity, smoothness, and a lingering aftertaste.

3. Correct answer: B) El Salvador

Description: El Salvadoran coffee is similar to Mexican coffee, featuring medium acidity, body, and aroma, with a soft taste that quickly dissipates.

4. Correct answer: D) Ethiopia

Description: Ethiopian coffee is famous for its good acidity, fruity flavor, and balanced body.

5. Correct answer: A) Brazil

Description: Brazilian coffee is known for being sweeter and having lower acidity than other Central American varieties.

6. Correct answer: B) Guatemala

Description: Guatemalan coffee is distinguished by its medium body, good acidity, slightly bitter chocolate flavor, and smoky undertone.

7. Correct answer: A) Hawaii

Description: Hawaiian coffee is known for its medium body, good acidity, and an excellent aftertaste that persists.

8. Correct answer: C) Honduras

Description: Honduran coffee is characterized by a medium aroma, medium acidity, and a weak body.

9. Correct answer: D) India

Description: Indian Monsoon coffee is recognized for its strong, pungent taste.

10. Correct answer: C) Indonesia

Description: Indonesian coffee is characterized by its full body, low acidity, and a slight earth and tree fragrance that lingers.

11. Correct answer: B) Sumatra - Indonesia

Description: Sumatra coffee is known for its strong body, very low acidity, and a touch of bitterness, with a lingering sweet grass aftertaste.

12. Correct answer: D) Kenya

Description: Kenyan coffee is known for its high acidity, strong fragrance, medium body, and fruity aftertaste.

13. Correct answer: B) Mexico

Description: Mexican coffee is characterized by a medium body, medium acidity, and a nutty flavor.

14. Correct answer: D) Panama

Description: Panamanian coffee is balanced with good acidity and a full body, complemented by fruity sweetness.

15. Correct answer: B) Peru

Description: Peruvian coffee is noted for its high aroma, medium acidity, medium body, and fruity notes.

16. Correct answer: A) Tanzania

Description: Tanzanian coffee is typically African, featuring a medium body and strong acidity.

17. Correct answer: C) Uganda

Description: Ugandan Robusta coffee is known for its vigorous character, full body, lively acidity, and unique sweetness.

18. Correct answer: D) Vietnam

Description: Vietnamese coffee is characterized by its low acidity and strong aroma.

19. Correct answer: A) Yemen

Description: Yemeni coffee is known for its strong body, high acidity, rich aroma, fruity and chocolatey notes, and a touch of bitterness.

20. Correct answer: A) Colombian Supremo

Description: Colombian Supremo coffee is known for its richness, well-balanced nature, medium to full body, mild sweetness, good acidity, and pleasant aroma.

21. Correct answer: A) Guatemalan Huehuetenango

Description: Guatemalan Huehuetenango coffee is known for its subtle and mild fruit flavors, light body, sweet fragrance, and a clean, lingering finish.

22. Correct answer: B) Yemen Mocha

Description: Yemen Mocha coffee is complex, deep, and earthy, with pungent notes of dry cinnamon, cardamom, and dried fruits.

23. Correct answer: D) Ethiopian Yirgacheffe

Description: Ethiopian Yirgacheffe coffee is bright, medium to light-bodied, with with fruity berry undertones and distinct floral notes in the aroma.

24. Correct answer: C) Sumatra Mandheling

Description: Sumatra Mandheling coffee is known for its complex, intense, and earthy flavors, smooth heavy body, sweet chocolate notes, low acidity, and a hint of licorice.

25. Correct answer: B) Guatemala Antigua Estela Plus

Description: Guatemala Antigua Estela Plus coffee is known for its well-balanced taste, dense body, flavors of pastries, plums, and cinnamon, rich aroma, and bright citrus acidity.

Notes:

....

....

....

....

....

....

....

....

....

....

....

....

....

....

....

....

....

....

....

....

....

....

3-A. Coffee Roasting

1. During the initial phase of roasting, _____ slightly increases, but after a brief period of heating, it diminishes and eventually almost vanishes.

    A. Acidity

    B. Body

    C. Aroma

    D. Flavor

2. _____ intensifies during the roasting process but diminishes as the beans become very dark.

    A. Acidity

    B. Body

    C. Aroma

    D. Flavor

3. When roasting, once the beans' temperature exceeds _____, the liquids within begin to boil, releasing steam.

    A. 140°F (60°C)

    B. 176°F (80°C)

    C. 212°F (100°C)

    D. 248°F (120°C)

4. The sugars in the coffee beans start to melt and caramelize at around _____ degrees.

    A. 212°F (100°C)

    B. 340°F (170°C)

    C. 176°F (80°C)

    D. 140°F (60°C)

5. The roasting stage where the beans reach an internal temperature of 375-400°F (190-205°C) and the silver skin dries and flakes off is known as _____.

    A. First stage

    B. Cinnamon stage

    C. American stage

    D. Last stage

6. At the American roasting stage, the temperature continues to climb, and at approximately _____, the beans start to crack.

    A. 390-420°F (199-215°C)

    B. 302-338°F (150-170°C)

    C. 356-374°F (180-190°C)

    D. 428-464°F (220-240°C)

7. During which roasting stage does the volume of the beans increase to about 60% larger than their original size?

    A. First stage

    B. Cinnamon stage

    C. American stage

    D. Last stage

8. At the _____ stage of roasting, the temperature reaches 425-430°F (220-225°C), and most of the beans have cracked.

    A. First stage

    B. Cinnamon stage

    C. American stage

    D. City Roast

9. At the _____ stage of roasting, the temperature ranges from 430-455°F (221-235°C).

    A. City

    B. Cinnamon

    C. Full City Roast

    D. American

10. The stage of roasting when beans begin to exude oil through their skin, accompanied by a slight popping sound, is called _____.

    A. Cinnamon stage

    B. American stage

    C. City Roast

    D. Full City Roast

11. At which stage of roasting do the beans lose about 12% of their original weight?

    A. Cinnamon stage

    B. American stage

    C. City Roast

    D. Full City Roast

12. At which stage of roasting do the beans lose about 17% of their original weight?

    A. Cinnamon stage

    B. American stage

    C. City Roast

    D. Full City Roast

13. During roasting, as the sugars caramelize, the sweetness of the beans increases, but as the caramel burns, the sweetness turns into _____.

    A. Bitterness

    B. Sourness

    C. Saltiness

    D. Tartness

14. Aroma increases during roasting but begins to decline as the roasted beans become _____.

    A. Light brown

    B. Grey

    C. Yellow

    D. Very dark

15. At the Cinnamon stage, _____ reaches its peak.

    A. Acidity

    B. Body

    C. Flavor

    D. Aroma

16. At which roasting stage are the beans dry, have doubled in size, have maximum aroma, and maintain high acidity?

    A. First stage

    B. Cinnamon stage

    C. American stage

    D. City Roast

17. At which roasting stage do the beans turn dark brown, and the acidity decreases while balancing with sweetness?

    A. First stage

    B. Cinnamon stage

    C. Full City Roast

    D. City Roast

18. At which stage of roasting do the beans lose about 20% of their original weight?

    A. American stage

    B. City Roast

    C. French/Italian Roast

    D. Full City Roast

19. At the stage of roasting where the temperature reaches 445-460°F (230-240°C), the beans start releasing oil and produce a significant amount of smoke.

    A. Cinnamon stage

    B. American stage

    C. City Roast

    D. Vienna Roast

20. During roasting, burnt oil is detected when the temperature reaches 460-475°F (240-245°C). The acidity fades, leaving only bitterness. This stage is referred to as _____.

    A. American stage

    B. City Roast

    C. French/Italian Roast

    D. Full City Roast

3-B. Coffee Roasting Questions Answers

1. Correct answer: A) Acidity

Description: Acidity in coffee rises a little at the start of the roasting process, but with further heating, it decreases and nearly disappears.

2. Correct answer: C) Aroma

Description: Aroma increases during roasting but starts to decline as the beans turn very dark.

3. Correct answer: C) 212°F (100°C)

Description: At temperatures above 212°F (100°C), the liquids inside the coffee beans start to boil, releasing steam.

4. Correct answer: B) 340°F (170°C)

Description: Sugars within the coffee beans begin to melt and caramelize at approximately 340°F (170°C).

5. Correct answer: B. Cinnamon stage

Description: The Cinnamon stage is identified by the beans reaching 375-400°F (190-205°C), during which the silver skin dries up and falls off.

6. Correct answer: A) 390-420°F (199-215°C)

Description: At the American roasting stage, the beans begin to crack at temperatures around 390-420°F (199-215°C).

7. Correct answer: C) American stage

Description: During the American roasting stage, the volume of the beans expands to approximately 60% larger than their original size.

8. Correct answer: D) City Roast

Description: The City Roast stage is characterized by a temperature of 425-430°F (220-225°C), with most beans having cracked.

9. Correct answer: C) Full City Roast

Description: During the Full City Roast stage, the temperature ranges from 430-455°F (221-235°C).

10. Correct answer: D) Full City Roast

Description: The Full City Roast stage is when the beans start to release oil through their skin, with a slight popping sound.

11. Correct answer: B) American stage

Description: At the American roasting stage, beans lose approximately 12% of their original weight.

12. Correct answer: D) Full City Roast

Description: Beans lose around 17% of their original weight during the Full City Roast stage.

13. Correct answer: A) Bitterness

Description: As the sugars caramelize during roasting, the sweetness eventually turns into bitterness when the caramel burns.

14. Correct answer: D) Very dark

Description: Aroma increases during roasting but starts to decrease as the beans turn very dark.

15. Correct answer: A) Acidity

Description: Acidity is at its highest during the Cinnamon stage of roasting.

16. Correct answer: D) City Roast

Description: In the City Roast stage, the beans are dry, have doubled in volume, have maximum aroma, and still possess high acidity.

17. Correct answer: C) Full City Roast

Description: During the Full City Roast stage, the beans become dark brown, with acidity decreasing and balancing with sweetness.

18. Correct answer: C) French/Italian Roast

Description: Beans lose around 20% of their original weight at the French/Italian Roast stage.

19. Correct answer: D) Vienna Roast

Description: At the Vienna Roast stage, beans begin to release oil and emit a lot of smoke when the temperature reaches 445-460°F (230-240°C).

20. Correct answer: C) French/Italian Roast

Description: The French/Italian Roast stage is marked by burnt oil, a disappearance of acidity, and the dominance of bitterness when the temperature hits 460-475°F (240-245°C).

Notes:

....
....
....
....
....
....
....
....
....
....
....
....
....
....

4-A. Coffee Taste

1. _____ refers to the person who identifies the actual taste of coffee by comparing it to the four basic tastes we recognize.

    A. Taster

    B. Cupper

    C. Taste Assessor

    D. Flavorist

2. _____ is the most important coffee taste or mouthfeel, describing the coffee's sharpness and freshness under the tongue and in the mouth.

    A. Acidity

    B. Body

    C. Aroma

    D. Flavor

3. _____ is the pleasing scent associated with coffee.

    A. Acidity

    B. Body

    C. Aroma

    D. Flavor

4. _____ refers to the taste that remains in the mouth after the acidity, aroma, and body have subsided.

    A. Aroma

    B. Flavor

    C. Aftertaste

    D. Body

5. In coffee tasting, what does the term "Complexity" refer to?

A. The amount of bitterness in the coffee

B. The range and depth of flavors that can be detected in the coffee

C. The texture of the coffee

D. The overall strength of the coffee

6. What does the term "Balance" signify in relation to a coffee's flavor profile?

A. The coffee has an even level of sweetness throughout.

B. No single characteristic (acidity, bitterness, sweetness, etc.) overpowers the flavor.

C. The coffee has a high level of bitterness.

D. The coffee is overly sweet.

7. What does the term "Bright" suggest about a coffee's flavor profile?

A. The coffee has a heavy body.

B. The coffee is low in acidity and sweetness.

C. The coffee has prominent and vibrant acidic notes.

D. The coffee has a dull and flat flavor.

8. In coffee tasting, what does "Body" refer to?

A. The level of bitterness in the coffee.

B. The texture and thickness of the coffee experienced in the mouth.

C. The aroma released during brewing.

D. The level of acidity in the coffee.

9. Which term is used to describe coffee that lacks flavor or has a dull taste?

    A. Bitter

    B. Bland

    C. Bright

    D. Juicy

10. The terms used to describe the level of acidity in coffee include _____.

    A. Bright, Tart

    B. Delicate, Intense

    C. Delicate, Intense, Poor, Soft

    D. Soft, Poor

11. The terms used to describe coffee aroma are _____.

    A. Fruity, Spicy

    B. Floral

    C. Earthy, Smoky

    D. Juicy, Spicy, Floral, Earthy, Smoky

12. The terms that best describe coffee flavor include _____.

    A. Piquant, Chocolaty

    B. Fruity, Flowery

    C. Piquant, Chocolaty, Fruity, Flowery

    D. Nutty, Sweet

13. The terms used to describe a bad coffee taste are _____.

A. Heartburn, Bitter

B. Piquant, Chocolaty, Fruity, Flowery

C. Musty, Moldy, Old

D. Heartburn, Bitter, Old, Musty, Moldy

14. After _____ hours, coffee loses approximately 50% of its aroma.

A. 6 hours

B. 8 hours

C. 5 hours

D. 10 hours

15. _____ refers to the lingering taste that remains in the mouth after swallowing coffee.

A. Aroma

B. Flavor

C. Aftertaste

D. Flowery

4-B. Coffee Taste Questions Answers

1. Correct answer: B) Cupper

Description: A Cupper is responsible for describing the actual taste of coffee by comparing it to the four basic tastes.

2. Correct answer: A) Acidity

Description: Acidity is a key coffee taste or mouthfeel, indicating the sharpness and freshness of coffee under the tongue and in the mouth.

3. Correct answer: C) Aroma

Description: Aroma is the term used to describe the pleasant scent of coffee.

4. Correct answer: B) Flavor

Description: Flavor is the taste left in the mouth after the acidity, aroma, and body have been neutralized.

5. Correct answer: B) The range and depth of flavors that can be detected in the coffee.

Description: Complexity in coffee refers to the range of flavors that can be identified in the coffee.

6. Correct answer: B) No single characteristic (acidity, bitterness, sweetness, etc.) overpowers the flavor.

Description: Balance in coffee flavor indicates that no single characteristic, such as acidity, bitterness, or sweetness, dominates the overall flavor.

7. Correct answer: C) The coffee has prominent and vibrant acidic notes.

Description: "Bright" refers to coffee with prominent and vibrant acidic notes.

8. Correct answer: B) The texture and thickness of the coffee experienced in the mouth.

Description: "Body" describes the texture and thickness of the coffee as it is experienced in the mouth.

9. Correct answer: B) Bland

Description: "Bland" is the term used to describe coffee that lacks flavor or has a dull taste.

10. Correct answer: C) Delicate, Intense, Poor, Soft

Description: Terms to describe the acidity level in coffee include Delicate, Intense, Poor, and Soft.

11. Correct answer: D) Juicy, Spicy, Floral, Earthy, Smoky.

Description: Terms used to describe coffee aroma include Fruity, Spicy, Floral, Earthy, and Smoky.

12. Correct answer: C) Piquant, Chocolaty, Fruity, Flowery

Description: The best descriptions of coffee flavor include piquant, chocolaty, fruity, and flowery.

13. Correct answer: D) Heartburn, Bitter, Old, Musty, Moldy

Description: Terms for describing a bad coffee taste include heartburn, bitter, old, musty, and moldy.

14. Correct answer: D) 10

Description: Coffee loses about 50% of its aroma after 10 hours.

15. Correct answer: C) Aftertaste

Description: Aftertaste is the lingering flavor that remains in the mouth after swallowing coffee.

Notes:

....
....
....
....
....
....
....
....
....
....
....
....
....
....
....
....
....
....
....
....
....
....
....
....
....
....
....
....
....

5-A. Coffee Grinding

1. Which type of grinder is typically recommended for achieving a consistent grind size?

A. Blade Grinder

B. Burr Grinder

C. Mortar and Pestle

D. Food Processor

2. At which grind level is the texture of the ground beans similar to white sugar, making it suitable for French press and filter coffee?

A. Coarse

B. Medium

C. Fine

D. Very Fine

3. At which grind level is the texture of the ground beans similar to table salt, making it suitable for Moka Pot and vacuum coffee?

A. Coarse

B. Medium

C. Fine

D. Very Fine

4. Which grind size is considered best for pour-over coffee?

A. Coarse

B. Medium

C. Fine

D. Very Fine

5. At which grind level is the texture of the ground beans similar to ground black pepper, making it suitable for Espresso?

    A. Coarse

    B. Medium

    C. Fine

    D. Very Fine

6. At which grind level is the texture of the ground beans like powder, making it suitable for Turkish coffee?

    A. Coarse

    B. Medium

    C. Fine

    D. Very Fine

7. Higher water pressure during brewing requires a _____ grind.

    A. Finer

    B. Coarser

    C. Medium

    D. Harsher

8. AeroPress requires a _____ grind.

    A. Coarse

    B. Medium

    C. Very Fine

    D. Coarse-Medium

9. What type of grind is typically used for cold brew coffee, which involves a longer extraction time?

A. Coarse

B. Medium

C. Fine

D. Very Fine

10. Which coffee brewing method generally does not require a very fine grind?

A. Turkish Coffee

B. Espresso

C. French Press

D. Aeropress

11. What effect does a coarser grind have on brewing time?

A. Shorter Brewing Time

B. Longer Brewing Time

C. No Effect

D. Variable Effect

12. At which grind level does a single bean produce an average of 200-1000 particles?

A. Coarse

B. Medium

C. Fine

D. Very Fine

13. At which grind level does a single bean produce an average of 1000-2000 particles?

A. Coarse

B. Medium

C. Fine

D. Very Fine

14. At which grind level does a single bean produce an average of 3000-4000 particles?

A. Coarse

B. Medium

C. Fine

D. Very Fine

15. At which grind level does a single bean produce an average of 15,000-35,000 particles?

A. Coarse

B. Medium

C. Fine

D. Very Fine

5-B. Coffee Grinding Questions Answers

1. Correct answer: B) Burr Grinder

Description: A Burr Grinder is generally recommended for producing a consistent grind size.

2. Correct answer: A) Coarse

Description: A coarse grind, similar in texture to white sugar, is ideal for French press and filter coffee.

3. Correct answer: B) Medium

Description: A medium grind, with a texture resembling table salt, is appropriate for Moka Pot and vacuum coffee.

4. Correct answer: B) Medium

Description: A medium grind is considered the best option for pour-over coffee.

5. Correct answer: C) Fine

Description: A fine grind, resembling ground black pepper, is suitable for Espresso.

6. Correct answer: D) Very Fine

Description: A very fine grind, similar to powder, is ideal for Turkish coffee.

7. Correct answer: A) Finer

Description: Higher water pressure requires a finer grind for optimal extraction.

8. Correct answer: B) Medium

Description: AeroPress is best prepared with a medium grind, allowing for a balanced extraction and smooth flavor.

9. Correct answer: A) Coarse

Description: A coarse grind is typically used for cold brew coffee, which requires a longer extraction time.

10. Correct answer: C) French Press

Description: A very fine grind is typically not recommended for French Press brewing.

11. Correct answer: B) Longer Brewing Time

Description: A coarser grind results in a longer brewing time.

12. Correct answer: A) Coarse

Description: At a coarse grind level, a single bean produces an average of 200-1000 particles.

13. Correct answer: B) Medium

Description: At a medium grind level, a single bean produces an average of 1000-2000 particles.

14. Correct answer: C) Fine

Description: At a fine grind level, a single bean produces an average of 3000-4000 particles.

15. Correct answer: D) Very Fine

Description: At a very fine grind level, a single bean produces an average of 15,000-35,000 particles.

Notes:

....

....

....

....

....

6-A. Coffee Caffeine Level

**1. The caffeine content in a 1 Oz (30 ml) Espresso coffee cup is
_____.**

    A. 60-80 mg

    B. 150-170 mg

    C. 180-200 mg

    D. 210-230 mg

**2. The caffeine content in a small 3 Oz (90 ml) Turkish coffee cup is
_____.**

    A. 60-90 mg

    B. 150-170 mg

    C. 180-200 mg

    D. 210-230 mg

**3. The caffeine content in a 6 Oz (180 ml) French press coffee cup is
_____.**

    A. 60-140 mg

    B. 150-170 mg

    C. 60-100 mg

    D. 210-230 mg

**4. The caffeine content in a 6 Oz (180 ml) filtered coffee cup is
_____.**

    A. 60-140 mg

    B. 150-170 mg

    C. 50-150 mg

    D. 60-100 mg

5. The caffeine content in a 6 Oz (180 ml) instant coffee cup is _____.

A. 30-90 mg

B. 150-170 mg

C. 50-150 mg

D. 40-130 mg

6. The caffeine content in a 6 Oz (180 ml) decaf coffee cup is _____.

A. 8-10 mg

B. 2-5 mg

C. 20-30 mg

D. 40-80 mg

7. The caffeine content in a 5 Oz (150 ml) Red Bull can is _____.

A. 35-40 mg

B. 45-50 mg

C. 55-60 mg

D. 70-80 mg

8. The caffeine content in a 5 Oz (150 ml) cola glass is _____.

A. 30-120 mg

B. 2-5 mg

C. 2-20 mg

D. 15-30 mg

9. The caffeine content in a 5 Oz (150 ml) bagged tea glass is _____.

A. 30-90 mg

B. 2-5 mg

C. 25-70 mg

D. 15-30 mg

10. The caffeine content in a 5 Oz (150 ml) green tea glass is _____.

    A. 30-90 mg

    B. 2-5 mg

    C. 25-70 mg

    D. 20-60 mg

11. The caffeine content in a 100 ml chocolate drink is _____.

    A. 50-90 mg

    B. 5-35 mg

    C. 40-70 mg

    D. 80-85 mg

12. Which type of coffee usually has the highest caffeine content?

    A. Espresso

    B. Drip coffee

    C. Americano

    D. Cold brew

13. What is the medical name for caffeine?

    A. Trimethylxanthine

    B. Tryptamine

    C. Glucose

    D. Methylene

14. Which sleep-inducing chemical does caffeine block from binding to nerve cells?

    A. Dopamine

    B. Oxytocin

    C. Adenosine

    D. Cholesterol

15. Which neurotransmitter or chemical messenger does caffeine stimulate?

    A. Dopamine

    B. Epinephrine

    C. Serotonin

    D. Glucose

6-B. Coffee Caffeine Level Questions Answers

1. Correct answer: A) 60-80 mg

Description: An Espresso coffee cup containing 1 Oz (30 ml) typically has 60-80 mg of caffeine.

2. Correct answer: A) 60-90 mg

Description: A small Turkish coffee cup of 3 Oz (90 ml) generally contains 60-90 mg of caffeine.

3. Correct answer: C) 60-100 mg

Description: A French press coffee cup containing 6 Oz (180 ml) usually has 60-100 mg of caffeine.

4. Correct answer: D) 60-100 mg

Description: A filtered coffee cup with 6 Oz (180 ml) generally contains 60-100 mg of caffeine.

5. Correct answer: A) 30-90 mg

Description: An instant coffee cup of 6 Oz (180 ml) typically contains 30-90 mg of caffeine.

6. Correct answer: B) 2-5 mg

Description: An instant decaf coffee cup of 6 Oz (180 ml) generally contains 2-5 mg of caffeine.

7. Correct answer: D) 70-80 mg

Description: A 5 Oz (150 ml) Red Bull can typically contains 70-80 mg of caffeine.

8. Correct answer: D) 15-30 mg

Description: A cola glass of 5 Oz (150 ml) generally contains 15-30 mg of caffeine.

9. Correct answer: C) 25-70 mg

Description: A bagged tea glass of 5 Oz (150 ml) usually contains 25-70 mg of caffeine.

10. Correct answer: D) 20-60 mg

Description: A green tea glass of 5 Oz (150 ml) typically contains 20-60 mg of caffeine.

11. Correct answer: B) 5-35 mg

Description: A chocolate drink of 100 ml generally contains 5-35 mg of caffeine.

12. Correct answer: D) Cold brew

Description: The Cold brew contains the highest amount of caffeine.

13. Correct answer: A) Trimethylxanthine

Description: The medical name for caffeine is Trimethylxanthine.

14. Correct answer: C) Adenosine

Description: Caffeine blocks adenosine, a sleep-inducing chemical, from binding to nerve cells.

15. Correct answer: A) Dopamine

Description: Caffeine stimulates dopamine, a neurotransmitter, or chemical messenger.

Notes:

....

....

....

....

....

....

7-A. Coffee Fruits Processing

1. The method where beans are placed in water, allowing spoiled cherries to float to the surface and be removed, is known as _____.

    A. Wet or Washed process

    B. Dry or Unwashed process

    C. Honey or Semi-washed process

    D. Honey and dry

2. The method where cherries are laid out in the sun to dry on a clean, thick surface is called _____.

    A. Wet or Washed process

    B. Dry or Unwashed process

    C. Honey or Semi-washed process

    D. Honey and dry

3. The process in which berries are dried without fully removing the mucilage layer, allowing the beans to absorb its flavor, is known as _____.

    A. Wet or Washed process

    B. Dry or Unwashed process

    C. Honey or Semi-washed process

    D. Honey and dry

4. How long do cherries typically take to dry during the coffee processing?

    A. 5 to 8 days

    B. 8 to 10 days

    C. 2 to 3 weeks

    D. 4 to 5 weeks

5. The Unwashed (Dry) process is also known as _____ processing.

A. Panama

B. Practical

C. International

D. Natural

6. Which coffee processing method is known for producing beans with a more pronounced fruity and complex flavor?

A. Wet (Washed) process

B. Dry (Natural) process

C. Honey process

D. Semi-washed process

7. Which coffee processing method results in a lighter body and cleaner taste?

A. Dry (Natural) process

B. Wet (Washed) process

C. Honey process

D. Semi-washed process

8. In coffee processing, what does "parchment" refer to?

A. The outer shell of the coffee cherry

B. The layer surrounding the coffee bean after removal from the cherry

C. The final roasted coffee bean

D. The paper used in drying beans

9. The most common method to assess coffee quality is _____.

A. Measuring the amount of defective materials in the coffee sample

B. Evaluating its aroma

C. Tasting the coffee flavor

D. Assessing aroma, flavor, and the number of defective beans

10. Coffee bean sizes on a sieve are measured in fractions of an inch. If a size is described as "size 17," what does this measurement represent?

A. 17/64"

B. 17/46"

C. 17/86"

D. 17/60"

11. Growers use the term _____ to describe the altitude of a coffee plantation.

A. Bean severity

B. Bean hardness

C. Bean firmness

D. Bean rigidity

12. Which altitude range is considered for Strictly Hard Beans (SHB)?

A. 4,000-4,500 ft (1,200-1,350 m)

B. 2,600-4,000 ft (1,100-1,200 m)

C. Above 4,500 ft (1,350 m)

D. 2,000-2,600 ft (600-800 m)

13. Which altitude range is typical for Hard Beans (HB)?

    A. 4,000-4,500 ft (1,200-1,350 m)

    B. 2,600-4,000 ft (1,100-1,200 m)

    C. 2,000-2,600 ft (600-800 m)

    D. Above 4,500 ft (1,350 m)

14. Which altitude range is associated with Semi-Hard Beans?

    A. 4,000-4,500 ft (1,200-1,350 m)

    B. 2,000-2,600 ft (600-800 m)

    C. 2,600-4,000 ft (1,100-1,200 m)

    D. Above 4,500 ft (1,350 m)

15. In some countries, a coffee screen size of _____ or larger is considered the best, while in others, it may be rated only as good.

    A. 16

    B. 14

    C. 17

    D. 12

7-B. Coffee Fruits Processing Questions Answers

1. Correct answer: A) Wet or Washed process

Description: The Wet or Washed process involves submerging beans in water to remove spoiled cherries that float to the surface.

2. Correct answer: B) Dry or Unwashed process

Description: The Dry or Unwashed process involves drying cherries in the sun on a clean, thick surface.

3. Correct answer: C) Honey or Semi-washed process

Description: The Honey or Semi-washed process involves drying berries while leaving some mucilage on, which the beans absorb for flavor.

4. Correct answer: C) 2 to 3 weeks

Description: Cherries generally take about 2 to 3 weeks to dry.

5. Correct answer: D) Natural

Description: The Unwashed (Dry) process is referred to as Natural processing.

6. Correct answer: B) Dry (Natural) process

Description: The Dry (Natural) process is recognized for producing beans with a more pronounced fruity and complex flavor.

7. Correct answer: B) Wet (Washed) process

Description: The Wet (Washed) process results in a lighter body and a cleaner taste.

8. Correct answer: B) The layer surrounding the coffee bean after removal from the cherry

Description: "Parchment" refers to the layer that surrounds the coffee bean after it is removed from the cherry.

9. Correct answer: D) Assessing aroma, flavor, and the number of defective beans.

Description: The most common method to determine coffee quality involves evaluating the aroma, flavor, and number of defective beans.

10. Correct answer: A) 17/64"

Description: Coffee bean sizes are measured using the unit 1/64 inch on a sieve. A size 17 screen indicates that the beans are 17/64 inch (about 6.75 mm) in diameter.

11. Correct answer: B) Bean hardness

Description: The term bean hardness is used by growers to grade the altitude of a coffee plantation.

12. Correct answer: C) Above 4,500 ft (1,350 m)

Description: Strictly Hard Beans (SHB) are classified as being grown at altitudes above 4,500 ft (1,350 m).

13. Correct answer: A) 4,000-4,500 ft (1,200-1,350 m)

Description: Hard Beans (HB) are typically grown at altitudes of 4,000-4,500 ft (1,200-1,350 m).

14. Correct answer: C) 2,600-4,000 ft (1,100-1,200 m)

Description: Semi-Hard Beans are typically grown at altitudes of 2,600-4,000 ft (1,100-1,200 m).

15. Correct answer: C) 17

Description: Coffee screen sizes of 17 and larger are considered top quality in some countries, though they may only be rated as good in others.

Notes: ....
....
....

8-A. Coffee Testing

1. The procedure used to assess and classify green coffee beans based on their quality is known as _____.

    A. Cupping

    B. Roasting

    C. Filtering

    D. Draining

2. For cupping, the coffee beans are roasted to which level?

    A. Full City Roast (430-455°F) (221-235°C)

    B. Vienna Roast (445-465°F) (230-240°C)

    C. City Roast (410-435°F) (210-224°C)

    D. American Roast 390-420°F (199-215°C)

3. The thin layer of ground coffee particles that floats on the surface of the liquid is referred to as _____.

    A. Surface

    B. Foam

    C. Skim

    D. Crust

4. The stage when the cup is brought to the nose for smelling is called _____.

    A. Before the break

    B. After the break

    C. Dry coffee aroma

    D. Filtering

5. The impression of the bouquet recorded when the cupper smells the ground coffee sample is termed as _____.

    A. Before the break

    B. After the break

    C. Dry coffee aroma

    D. Crust

6. The stage of breaking the crust, which releases a strong coffee aroma, is referred to as _____.

    A. Before the break

    B. After the break

    C. Dry coffee aroma

    D. Spicy

7. What should be the temperature of the water used in cupping?

    A. 160-170°F (71-77°C)

    B. 180-190°F (82-88°C)

    C. 200-205°F (93-96°C)

    D. 210-215°F (99-102°C)

8. What kind of container is most commonly used for cupping coffee?

    A. Tall glass

    B. Mug

    C. Small ceramic cup

    D. Metal bowl

9. How long should coffee grounds steep in hot water during cupping before breaking the crust?

    A. 1-2 minutes

    B. 3-5 minutes

    C. 5-7 minutes

    D. 7-10 minutes

10. What is the purpose of "breaking the crust" during cupping?

    A. To release the coffee oils

    B. To mix the coffee grounds

    C. To evaluate the coffee's aroma and flavors

    D. To cool the coffee

11. The method known as the Three "S's" stands for _____.

    A. "Smell, Swirl, and Sip"

    B. "Swirl, Sip, and Swallow"

    C. "Smell, Slurp, and Spit"

    D. "Savor, Smell, and Sip"

12. One of the best ways to demonstrate the wide range of Espresso flavors is through the _____.

    A. 2 Cup Espresso Flavor Experiment

    B. 4 Cup Espresso Flavor Experiment

    C. 8 Cup Espresso Flavor Experiment

    D. 6 Cup Espresso Flavor Experiment

13. Cuppers typically use a flat, wide spoon made of _____.

A. Non-reactive metal

B. Reactive metal

C. Wood

D. Wood and copper

14. For cupping, the coffee beans are ground _____.

A. Extra fine

B. Fine

C. Medium

D. Coarsely

15. What is a key benefit of allowing coffee grounds to "bloom" before cupping?

A. It helps in the even distribution of coffee grounds

B. It releases carbon dioxide and enhances flavor clarity

C. It cools down the coffee to an ideal-tasting temperature

D. It mixes the coffee oils more thoroughly

8-B. Coffee Testing Questions Answers

1. Correct answer: A) Cupping

Description: Cupping is the procedure used to classify green coffee beans and confirm their quality.

2. Correct answer: C) City Roast (410-435°F) (210-224°C)

Description: Coffee beans for cupping are roasted to a City Roast, ranging from 410-435°F (210-224°C).

3. Correct answer: D) Crust

Description: The thin layer of ground coffee particles floating on the surface of the liquid is known as the crust.

4. Correct answer: A) Before the break

Description: The stage when the cupper brings the cup to the nose to smell is called "before the break."

5. Correct answer: C) Dry coffee aroma

Description: The dry coffee aroma is the bouquet impression recorded when smelling the ground coffee sample.

6. Correct answer: B) After the break

Description: The aroma released after breaking the crust is called "after the break."

7. Correct answer: C) 200-205°F (93-96°C)

Description: The water used for cupping should be between 200-205°F (93-96°C).

8. Correct answer: C) Small ceramic cup

Description: A small ceramic cup is typically used for cupping coffee.

9. Correct answer: B) 3-5 minutes

Description: Coffee grounds should steep in hot water for 3-5 minutes before breaking the crust.

10. Correct answer: C) To evaluate the coffee's aroma and flavors

Description: The purpose of breaking the crust during cupping is to evaluate the coffee's aroma and flavors.

11. Correct answer: C) "Smell, Slurp, and Spit"

Description: The Three "S's" method stands for "Smell, Slurp, and Spit."

12. Correct answer: B) 4 Cup Espresso Flavor Experiment

Description: The 4 Cup Espresso Flavor Experiment is one of the best methods to demonstrate the wide range of Espresso flavors.

13. Correct answer: A) Non-reactive metal

Description: Cuppers typically use a flat, wide spoon made of non-reactive metal.

14. Correct answer: D) Coarsely

Description: For cupping, coffee beans are ground coarsely.

15. Correct answer: B) It releases carbon dioxide and enhances flavor clarity

Description: Allowing coffee grounds to "bloom" before cupping releases carbon dioxide and enhances flavor clarity.

Notes: ....
....
....
....
....
....

9-A. Coffee Plant and Berries

1. How many years does it take for a coffee tree to start producing fruit?

    A. 1 to 2.5 years

    B. 3.5 to 4 years

    C. 5 to 6 years

    D. 7 to 8 years

2. What is the typical life span of a coffee tree?

    A. 10 to 12 years

    B. 20 to 25 years

    C. About 100 years

    D. About 200 years

3. How tall can coffee trees grow?

    A. 30 feet (about 9 m)

    B. 50 feet (about 15 m)

    C. 70 feet (about 21 m)

    D. 80 feet (about 24 m)

4. What are the two primary commercial coffee species produced worldwide?

    A. Arabica and Liberica

    B. Arabica and Plantation

    C. Robusta and Liberica

    D. Arabica and Robusta

5. Which coffee species is rare and economically insignificant?

   A. Arabica

   B. Robusta

   C. Liberica

   D. Both A and B

6. The fruit of the coffee tree, when ripe, is similar to a _____.

   A. Cranberry

   B. Cherry

   C. Blueberry

   D. Plum

7. How many layers cover the coffee beans inside the cherry?

   A. 10

   B. 9

   C. 4

   D. 7

8. The shiny greenish-yellow layer that covers the beans inside the coffee cherry is called _____.

   A. Mesocarp

   B. Exocarp

   C. Silver skin

   D. None of the above

9. What is the name of the second thin protective layer that surrounds the coffee bean?

    A. Exocarp

    B. Parchment

    C. Mesocarp

    D. Membrane

10. How are the flowers of the coffee plant best described?

    A. Red, bell-shaped, and scentless

    B. Yellow, round, and sweet-scented

    C. White, star-shaped, clustered, and fragrant

    D. Purple, tube-shaped, and bitter-scented

11. A coffee fruit that contains only a single coffee bean is called a _____.

    A. Peaberry

    B. Cherry

    C. Parchment

    D. Meaberry

12. Typically, about _____ of all coffee beans are peaberry.

    A. 15%

    B. 5%

    C. 20%

    D. 17%

13. Arabica coffee accounts for approximately _____ of global coffee production.

A. 30%

B. 44%

C. 65%

D. 80%

14. Which coffee species contains a lower amount of caffeine and has a rich taste?

A. Robusta

B. Arabica

C. Liberica

D. Both A and B

15. Arabica coffee is primarily grown in _____.

A. South America, Central America, and Eastern Africa

B. Europe and Asia

C. Australia and the Caribbean

D. North America and the Middle East

16. The two most common species of the Arabica coffee tree are _____.

A. Liberica and Typica

B. Plantation and Bourbon

C. Typica and Bourbon

D. Typica and Plantation

17. The Robusta coffee tree is primarily grown in _____.

    A. South America and Eastern Africa

    B. Asia and West Africa

    C. Australia

    D. North America

18. Which coffee varieties are more resistant to diseases and pests?

    A. Liberica

    B. Arabica

    C. Robusta

    D. Plantation

19. Compared to Arabica, how much more caffeine do Robusta coffee beans contain?

    A. Twice

    B. 3 times

    C. 4 times

    D. 5 times

20. The taste of Robusta coffee is generally _____.

    A. Caramel-like

    B. Bitter

    C. A little bit salty

    D. Sour

21. The taste of Arabica coffee is often described as _____.

A. Caramel-like

B. Acidic

C. Nutty

D. Bitter

22. How many pounds of cherries are required to produce 1 pound (0.45 kg) of coffee beans?

A. 1 pound (0.45 kg)

B. 3 pounds (1.3 kg)

C. 5 pounds (2.26 kg)

D. 7 pounds (3.17 kg)

23. When does the Arabica coffee plant typically start to bloom?

A. In Summer

B. In Winter

C. After the rainy season

D. In Autumn

24. When does the Robusta coffee plant typically start to bloom?

A. In Summer

B. Irregularly

C. After the rain

D. In Winter

25. How long does it take for the Arabica coffee plant to go from flowering to ripening?

A. 2 months

B. 5 months

C. 7 months

D. 9 months

26. How long does it take for the Robusta coffee plant to go from flowering to ripening?

A. 7 months

B. 9 months

C. 11 months

D. 2 years

27. What is the optimal altitude for growing the Arabica coffee tree?

A. 1,000-1,800 ft (300-550 m)

B. 2,600-6,500 ft (800-2,000 m)

C. 5,000-7,400 ft (1,524-2,255 m)

D. 8,000-9,500 ft (2,438-2,895 m)

28. What is the optimal altitude for growing the Robusta coffee tree?

A. 0-4,000 ft (0-1,219 m)

B. 4,400-5,600 ft (1,340-1,707 m)

C. 5,000-7,500 ft (1,524-2,286 m)

D. 7,000-8,300 ft (2,133-2,530 m)

29. Which coffee species requires more rainfall and can be grown at sea level?

> A. Arabica
>
> B. Liberica
>
> C. Robusta
>
> D. Augusta

30. Arabica beans are typically _____ and _____.

> A. Red and large
>
> B. Black and small
>
> C. Rectangular and elongated
>
> D. Small and tiny

31. Robusta beans are generally _____ and _____.

> A. Rectangular and elongated
>
> B. Round and rectangular
>
> C. Small and roundish
>
> D. Extra-large and rectangular

32. Which country is the world's leading producer of Robusta coffee beans?

> A. Vietnam
>
> B. Colombia
>
> C. Ethiopia
>
> D. Costa Rica

33. Which type of coffee requires partial shade for successful growth and cannot tolerate direct sunlight?

A. Robusta

B. Liberica

C. Arabica

D. Arabusta

34. Most of the best-tasting coffee is made from _____ beans.

A. Liberica

B. Robusta

C. Arabica

D. Arabusta

35. The quality of green (unroasted) coffee deteriorates slowly, so it must be stored at _____ temperature.

A. 70°F (20°C)

B. 86°F (30°C)

C. 104°F (40°C)

D. 122°F (50°C)

9-B. Coffee Plant and Berries Questions Answers

1. Correct answer: C) 5 to 6 years

Description: It takes a coffee tree about 5 to 6 years to start producing fruit.

2. Correct answer: B) 20 to 25 years

Description: The life span of a coffee tree is typically around 20 to 25 years.

3. Correct answer: A) 30 feet (about 9 m)

Description: Coffee trees can grow up to about 30 feet (9 meters) in height.

4. Correct answer: D) Arabica and Robusta

Description: The two main commercial coffee species produced globally are Arabica and Robusta.

5. Correct answer: C) Liberica

Description: Liberica is a coffee species that is rare and economically insignificant.

6. Correct answer: B) Cherry

Description: The fruit of the coffee tree, when ripe, is similar to a cherry in size, shape, and color.

7. Correct answer: C) 4

Description: Coffee beans inside the cherry are covered by four layers.

8. Correct answer: C) Silver skin

Description: The shiny greenish-yellow layer covering the beans inside the coffee cherry is known as the silver skin.

9. Correct answer: B) Parchment

Description: The parchment is the second thin protective layer surrounding the coffee bean.

10. Correct Answer: C) White, star-shaped, clustered, and fragrant

Description: Coffee plant flowers are white and star-shaped, growing in clusters of 8 to 15. They have a strong, pleasant fragrance.

11. Correct answer: A) Peaberry

Description: A coffee fruit containing only a single coffee bean is known as a peaberry.

12. Correct answer: B) 5%

Description: About 5% of all coffee beans are peaberry.

13. Correct answer: C) 65%

Description: Arabica coffee makes up about 65% of global coffee production.

14. Correct answer: B) Arabica

Description: Arabica coffee has a lower caffeine content and a rich taste.

15. Correct answer: A) South America, Central America, and Eastern Africa

Description: Arabica coffee is mainly grown in South America, Central America, and Eastern Africa.

16. Correct answer: C) Typica and Bourbon

Description: The two most common species of the Arabica coffee tree are Typica and Bourbon.

17. Correct answer: B. Asia and West Africa

Description: The Robusta coffee tree is mainly grown in Asia and West Africa.

18. Correct answer: C) Robusta

Description: Robusta coffee is more resistant to diseases compared to others.

19. Correct answer: A) Twice

Description: Robusta coffee beans almost contain double of the caffeine found in the Arabica beans.

20. Correct answer: B) Bitter

Description: The taste of Robusta coffee is typically bitter.

21. Correct answer: B) Acidic

Description: Arabica coffee is often described as having an acidic taste.

22. Correct answer: C) 5 pounds (2.26 kg)

Description: It takes about 5 pounds (2.26 kg) of cherries to produce 1 pound (0.45 kg) of coffee beans.

23. Correct answer: C) After the rainy season

Description: The Arabica coffee plant starts to bloom after the rainy season.

24. Correct answer: B) Irregularly

Description: The Robusta coffee plant blooms irregularly.

25. Correct answer: C) 9 months

Description: The Arabica coffee plant takes about 9 months from flowering to ripening.

26. Correct answer: C) 11 months

Description: The Robusta coffee plant takes about 11 months from flowering to ripening.

27. Correct answer: B) 2,600-6,500 ft (800-2,000 m)

Description: The optimal altitude for growing Arabica coffee is between 2,600 and 6,500 feet (800-2,000 meters).

28. Correct answer: A) 0-4,000 ft (0-1,219 m)

Description: The optimal altitude for growing Robusta coffee is between 0 and 4,000 feet (0-1,219 meters).

29. Correct answer: C) Robusta

Description: Robusta coffee requires more precipitation and can be grown at sea level.

30. Correct answer: C) Rectangular and elongated

Description: Arabica beans are rectangular and elongated in shape.

31. Correct answer: C) Small and roundish

Description: Robusta beans are small and round in shape.

32. Correct answer: A) Vietnam

Description: Vietnam is the world's leading producer of Robusta coffee beans.

33. Correct answer: C) Arabica

Description: Arabica coffee requires partial shade and cannot tolerate direct sunlight.

34. Correct answer: C) Arabica

Description: Most of the best-tasting coffee is made from Arabica beans.

35. Correct answer: A) 70°F (20°C)

Description: Green (unroasted) coffee must be stored at 70°F (20°C) to maintain its quality.

Notes:

....

....

....

....

....

....

....

....

....

....

....

....

....

....

....

....

....

....

....

....

....

....

....

....

....

10-A. Coffee History

1. The first coffee shop in Turkey was established in _____.

    A. 1475

    B. 1530

    C. 1601

    D. 1650

2. When was the first coffee shop in Italy opened?

    A. 1575

    B. 1645

    C. 1680

    D. 1700

3. The first coffee shop in Paris was opened in _____.

    A. 1672

    B. 1700

    C. 1753

    D. 1810

4. What was the name of the first coffee shop opened in England?

    A. Starbucks

    B. Caffeine

    C. Penny University

    D. Coffee Aroma

5. Where did coffee originally come from?

    A. South and Central America

    B. Hawaii

    C. Africa

    D. Asia

6. When was coffee brought to Brazil?

    A. 1670

    B. 1727

    C. 1800

    D. 1812

7. Which country is the largest producer of coffee in the world?

    A. Brazil

    B. Yemen

    C. Colombia

    D. Vietnam

8. Who is credited with patenting the modern percolator design in 1865?

    A. Carl Linnaeus

    B. Peter Smith

    C. James Mason

    D. Melitta Bentz

9. In 1890, _____ from New Zealand patented the first instant coffee, known as "soluble coffee."

    A. George Washington

    B. Alphonse Allais

    C. David Strang

    D. Louis Dapples

10. Where was the first prototype of the Espresso machine developed?

    A. Brazil

    B. France

    C. China

    D. Turkey

11. In what year was the first prototype of the Espresso machine developed?

    A. 1822

    B. 1900

    C. 1950

    D. 1994

12. Who introduced the first Espresso machine?

    A. Luigi Bezzera

    B. James Mason

    C. Peter Smith

    D. Renato Bialetti

13. The first Espresso machine was introduced in which year?

A. 1880

B. 1900

C. 1901

D. 1840

14. Who began commercially producing instant coffee?

A. Louis Dapples

B. Dr. Satori Kato

C. George Constant Washington

D. Angelo Moriondo

15. When did the commercial production of instant coffee begin?

A. 1909

B. 1950

C. 1995

D. 1930

16. Who designed the first Moka pot, which became widely used in Italy?

A. Louis Dapples

B. Alfonso Bialetti

C. George Washington

D. Melitta Bentz

17. When was the first Moka pot designed, eventually becoming common in more than 90% of Italian homes?

    A. 1933

    B. 1950

    C. 1975

    D. 1982

18. Which company introduced the E61 Espresso machine group head and the electric pump?

    A. Faema

    B. Baristas

    C. La Pavoni

    D. Rancilio

19. In what year did the Italian company Faema introduce the E61 Espresso machine group head and the electric pump?

    A. 1933

    B. 1950

    C. 1975

    D. 1961

20. Which company introduced the ESE (Easy Serving Espresso) pod that became the global standard?

    A. Baristas

    B. Illy

    C. La Pavoni

    D. Rancilio

10-B. Coffee History Questions Answers

1. Correct answer: A) 1475

Description: The first coffee shop in Turkey was opened in 1475.

2. Correct answer: B) 1645

Description: The first coffee shop in Italy was opened in 1645.

3. Correct answer: A) 1672

Description: The first coffee shop in Paris was opened in 1672.

4. Correct answer: C) Penny University

Description: The first coffee shop in England was called Penny University.

5. Correct answer: C) Africa

Description: Coffee originally came from Africa.

6. Correct answer: B) 1727

Description: Coffee was brought to Brazil in 1727.

7. Correct answer: A) Brazil

Description: Brazil is the world's largest coffee producer.

8. Correct answer: C) James Mason

Description: James Mason is credited with patenting the modern percolator design in 1865.

9. Correct answer: C) David Strang

Description: David Strang from New Zealand patented the first instant coffee in 1890.

10. Correct answer: B) France

Description: The first Espresso machine prototype was developed in France.

11. Correct answer: A) 1822

Description: The first Espresso machine prototype was developed in 1822.

12. Correct answer: A) Luigi Bezzera

Description: Luigi Bezzera introduced the first Espresso machine.

13. Correct answer: C) 1901

Description: The first Espresso machine was introduced in 1901.

14. Correct answer: C) George Constant Washington

Description: George Constant Washington, an American inventor, began commercially producing instant coffee.

15. Correct answer: A) 1909

Description: Commercial production of instant coffee began in 1909.

16. Correct answer: B) Alfonso Bialetti

Description: Alfonso Bialetti designed the first Moka pot.

17. Correct answer: A) 1933

Description: The first Moka pot was designed in 1933 and became prevalent in over 90% of Italian homes.

18. Correct answer: A) Faema

Description: Faema introduced the E61 Espresso machine group head and the electric pump.

19. Correct answer: D) 1961

Description: Faema introduced the E61 Espresso machine group head and electric pump in 1961.

20. Correct answer: B) Illy

Description: Illy introduced the ESE (Easy Serving Espresso) pod, which has become the worldwide standard.

Notes:

....
....
....
....
....
....
....
....
....
....
....
....
....
....
....
....
....
....
....
....
....

Conclusion

Congratulations on completing *The Ultimate Coffee Quiz Book*!
We hope you enjoyed testing your coffee knowledge and learned
something new along the way. Whether you aced every question or
found a few that stumped you, remember that the world of coffee
is vast and ever-evolving. Keep exploring, keep brewing, and keep
savoring every cup. Your journey through the world of coffee doesn't
end here—there's always more to discover and enjoy. Cheers to your
continued coffee adventures!

The End